Conten

Slow-Simmered Curried Chicken

1½ cups chopped onions

1 medium green bell pepper, chopped

1 pound boneless, skinless chicken breasts or thighs, cut into bite-size pieces

1 cup medium salsa

2 teaspoons grated fresh ginger

½ teaspoon garlic powder

½ teaspoon red pepper flakes

¼ cup chopped fresh cilantro

1 teaspoon sugar

1 teaspoon curry powder

¾ teaspoon salt

Hot cooked rice

1. Place onions and bell pepper in **CROCK-POT®** slow cooker. Place chicken on top.

2. Combine salsa, ginger, garlic powder and red pepper flakes in small bowl; spoon over chicken. Cover; cook on **LOW 5 to 6 hours** or until chicken is tender.

3. Combine cilantro, sugar, curry powder and salt in small bowl; stir into **CROCK-POT®** slow cooker. Cover; cook on **HIGH 15 minutes** or until heated through. Serve over rice.

makes 4 servings

Chicken Marsala with Fettuccine

4 boneless, skinless chicken breasts
Salt and black pepper
1 tablespoon vegetable oil
1 onion, chopped
½ cup Marsala wine
2 packages (6 ounces each) sliced brown mushrooms
½ cup chicken broth
2 teaspoons Worcestershire sauce
½ cup whipping cream
2 tablespoons cornstarch
8 ounces cooked fettuccine
2 tablespoons chopped fresh parsley (optional)

1. Coat **CROCK-POT®** slow cooker with nonstick cooking spray. Season chicken with salt and pepper. Transfer to **CROCK-POT®** slow cooker.

2. Heat oil in large skillet over medium heat. Add onion; cook and stir until translucent. Add wine; cook 2 to 3 minutes or until mixture reduces slightly. Stir in mushrooms. Add broth, Worcestershire sauce, ½ teaspoon salt and ½ teaspoon pepper. Pour mixture over chicken. Cover; cook on **HIGH 1½ to 1¾ hours** or until chicken is cooked through.

3. Remove chicken to cutting board. Cover loosely with foil; let stand 10 to 15 minutes. Stir cream and cornstarch in small bowl until smooth. Whisk into cooking liquid. Cover; cook on **HIGH 15 minutes** or until mixture is thickened. Season with salt and pepper.

4. Meanwhile, cook pasta according to directions on package. Drain and transfer to large serving bowl. Slice chicken breasts and place on pasta. Top with sauce and garnish with parsley.

makes 6 to 8 servings

Tip: Skinless chicken is usually best for recipes using the **CROCK-POT®** slow cooker because the skin can shrivel and curl during cooking.

Chicken Sausage with Peppers and Basil

1 tablespoon olive oil

½ yellow onion, minced (about ½ cup)

1 clove garlic, minced

1 pound sweet or hot Italian chicken sausage, casings removed and cut into 1-inch pieces

1 can (28 ounces) whole tomatoes, drained and seeded

½ red bell pepper, cut into ½-inch slices

½ yellow bell pepper, cut into ½-inch slices

½ orange bell pepper, cut into ½-inch slices

¾ cup chopped fresh basil

Red pepper flakes

Salt and black pepper

Hot cooked pasta

1. Heat oil in large skillet over medium heat. Add onion and garlic; cook and stir until onion is translucent.

2. Add sausage to skillet; cook 3 to 4 minutes or until just beginning to brown. Transfer to **CROCK-POT®** slow cooker with slotted spoon, skimming off some fat.

3. Add tomatoes, bell peppers, basil, red pepper flakes, salt and black pepper to **CROCK-POT®** slow cooker; stir to blend. Cover; cook on **HIGH 2½ to 3 hours** or until peppers have softened. Serve over pasta.

makes 4 servings

Tip: It's not necessary to brown meat before slow cooking. However, if you prefer the look and flavor of browned meat, don't skip this step.

Chicken in Enchilada Sauce

1   can (about 14 ounces) diced tomatoes with smoked chipotle chiles

1   can (10 ounces) enchilada sauce

1   cup frozen or canned corn

¼   teaspoon ground cumin

¼   teaspoon black pepper, or to taste

1½ pounds boneless, skinless chicken thighs, cut into bite-size pieces

2   tablespoons minced fresh cilantro

½   cup shredded pepper jack cheese**

    Sliced green onions (optional)

If tomatoes with smoked chipotle chiles aren't available, use diced tomatoes with chiles or plain diced tomatoes plus ¼ teaspoon crushed red pepper flakes.

**For a less spicy dish, use Monterey Jack cheese.*

1. Combine tomatoes, enchilada sauce, corn, cumin, and pepper in **CROCK-POT®** slow cooker. Add chicken; mix well to combine. Cover; cook on **LOW 6 to 7 hours.**

2. Stir in cilantro. Spoon chicken and sauce into four shallow bowls. Sprinkle each serving with 2 tablespoons cheese. Garnish with green onions.

makes 4 servings

Creamy Chicken and Mushrooms

  1 teaspoon salt

  ½ teaspoon black pepper

  ¼ teaspoon paprika

  3 boneless, skinless chicken breasts, cut into pieces

1½ cups sliced fresh mushrooms

  ½ cup sliced green onions

1¾ teaspoons chicken bouillon granules

  1 cup dry white wine

  ½ cup water

  1 can (5 ounces) evaporated milk

  5 teaspoons cornstarch

     Hot cooked rice

1. Combine salt, pepper and paprika in small bowl; sprinkle over chicken.

2. Layer chicken, mushrooms, green onions and bouillon in **CROCK-POT**® slow cooker. Pour wine and water over top. Cover; cook on **HIGH 3 hours** or on **LOW 5 to 6 hours.** Remove chicken and vegetables to platter. Tent with foil; let stand 10 to 15 minutes.

3. Combine evaporated milk and cornstarch in small saucepan, stirring until smooth. Add 2 cups cooking liquid from **CROCK-POT**® slow cooker; bring to a boil. Boil 1 minute or until thickened, stirring constantly. Serve chicken and sauce over rice.

makes 3 to 4 servings

Chicken and Spicy Black Bean Tacos

 1 can (15 ounces) black beans, rinsed and drained
 1 can (10 ounces) tomatoes with mild green chiles, drained
 1½ teaspoons chili powder
 ¾ teaspoon ground cumin
 1 tablespoon plus 1 teaspoon extra virgin olive oil, divided
 12 ounces boneless, skinless chicken breasts, rinsed and patted dry
 12 crisp corn taco shells
    Optional toppings: shredded lettuce, diced tomatoes, shredded cheese, sour cream, ripe olives

1. Coat **CROCK-POT®** slow cooker with nonstick cooking spray. Add beans and tomatoes. Blend chili powder and cumin with 1 teaspoon oil and rub onto chicken breasts. Place chicken in **CROCK-POT®** slow cooker. Cover; cook on **HIGH 1¾ hours.**

2. Remove chicken and slice. Transfer bean mixture to bowl using slotted spoon. Stir in 1 tablespoon oil.

3. To serve, warm taco shells according to package directions. Fill with equal amounts of bean mixture and chicken. Top as desired.

makes 4 servings

Citrus Mangoretto Chicken

4 boneless, skinless chicken breasts (about 1 pound)
1 large ripe mango, peeled and diced
3 tablespoons freshly squeezed lime juice
1 tablespoon grated lime peel
¼ cup amaretto liqueur
1 tablespoon chopped fresh rosemary *or*
  1 teaspoon crushed dried rosemary
1 cup chicken broth
1 tablespoon water
2 teaspoons cornstarch

1. Place 2 chicken breasts side by side on bottom of **CROCK-POT®** slow cooker.

2. Combine mango, lime juice, lime peel, amaretto and rosemary in medium bowl. Spread half of mango mixture over chicken in **CROCK-POT®** slow cooker. Lay remaining 2 chicken breasts on top crosswise, and spread with remaining mango mixture. Carefully pour broth around edges of chicken. Cover; cook on **LOW 3 to 4 hours.**

3. Stir water into cornstarch in small bowl. Whisk into cooking liquid. Cover; cook on **LOW 15 minutes** or until sauce has thickened. Serve mango and sauce over chicken.

makes 4 servings

Variation: For a refreshing change, chill the cooked chicken and sauce. Slice the chicken and serve it over salad greens, drizzling the sauce on top.

Greek Chicken and Orzo

2 medium green bell peppers, cut into thin strips
1 cup chopped onion
2 teaspoons extra virgin olive oil
8 chicken thighs, rinsed and patted dry
1 tablespoon dried oregano
½ teaspoon dried rosemary
½ teaspoon garlic powder
¾ teaspoon salt, divided
½ teaspoon black pepper, divided
8 ounces uncooked dry orzo pasta
  Juice and grated peel of 1 medium lemon
½ cup water
2 ounces crumbled feta cheese (optional)
  Chopped fresh parsley (optional)

1. Coat **CROCK-POT®** slow cooker with nonstick cooking spray. Add bell peppers and onion.

2. Heat oil in large skillet over medium-high heat. Brown chicken on both sides. Transfer to **CROCK-POT®** slow cooker, overlapping slightly if necessary. Sprinkle chicken with oregano, rosemary, garlic powder, ¼ teaspoon salt and ¼ teaspoon black pepper. Cover; cook on **LOW 5 to 6 hours** or on **HIGH 3 to 4 hours** or until chicken is tender.

3. Remove chicken to separate plate. Turn **CROCK-POT®** slow cooker to **HIGH.** Stir orzo, lemon juice, lemon peel, water, and remaining ½ teaspoon salt and ¼ teaspoon black pepper into **CROCK-POT®** slow cooker. Top with chicken. Cover; cook on **HIGH 30 minutes** or until pasta is heated through. Garnish with feta cheese and parsley.

makes 4 servings

Tip: Browning skin-on chicken not only adds flavor and color, but also prevents the skin from shrinking and curling during the long, slow cooking process.

Provençal Lemon and Olive Chicken

 2 **cups chopped onion**

 8 **skinless chicken thighs (about 2½ pounds)**

 1 **lemon, thinly sliced and seeds removed**

 1 **cup pitted green olives**

 1 **tablespoon olive brine from jar or white vinegar**

 2 **teaspoons herbes de Provence**

 1 **bay leaf**

½ **teaspoon salt**

⅛ **teaspoon black pepper**

 1 **cup chicken broth**

½ **cup minced fresh parsley**

1. Place onion in 4-quart **CROCK-POT**® slow cooker. Arrange chicken thighs over onion. Place lemon slice on each thigh. Add olives, brine, herbes de Provence, bay leaf, salt and pepper. Slowly pour in chicken broth.

2. Cover; cook on **LOW 5 to 6 hours** or on **HIGH 3 to 3½ hours** or until chicken is tender. Stir in parsley before serving.

makes 8 servings

Note: To skin chicken easily, grasp skin with paper towel and pull away. Repeat with fresh paper towel for each piece of chicken, discarding skins and towels.

Spicy Grits with Chicken

  4 cups chicken broth

  1 cup grits*

  1 jalapeño pepper, seeded and finely chopped**

  ½ teaspoon salt

  ¼ teaspoon paprika

  ¼ teaspoon black pepper

  ¾ cup shredded sharp Cheddar cheese

1½ cups chopped cooked chicken breast

  ½ cup half-and-half

  2 tablespoons chopped chives, plus additional for garnish

*You may use coarse, instant, yellow or stone-ground grits.

**Jalapeño peppers can sting and irritate the skin, so wear rubber gloves when handling peppers and do not touch your eyes.

1. Combine broth, grits, jalapeño pepper, salt, paprika and black pepper in **CROCK-POT®** slow cooker. Stir well. Cover; cook on **LOW 4 hours.**

2. Add cheese and stir until melted. Stir in chicken, half-and-half and 2 tablespoons chives. Add salt and pepper, if desired. Cover; cook on **LOW 15 minutes** to blend flavors. Garnish with additional chives.

makes 6 servings

Country Captain Chicken

4 boneless, skinless chicken thighs

2 tablespoons all-purpose flour

2 tablespoons vegetable oil, divided

1 cup chopped green bell pepper

1 large onion, chopped

1 rib celery, chopped

1 clove garlic, minced

¼ cup chicken broth

2 cups canned crushed tomatoes or diced fresh tomatoes

½ cup golden raisins

1½ teaspoons curry powder

1 teaspoon salt

¼ teaspoon paprika

¼ teaspoon black pepper

Hot cooked rice

Fresh Italian parsley (optional)

1. Coat chicken with flour; set aside. Heat 1 tablespoon oil in large skillet over medium-high heat. Add bell pepper, onion, celery and garlic; cook and stir 5 minutes or until vegetables are tender. Place vegetables in **CROCK-POT®** slow cooker.

2. Heat remaining 1 tablespoon oil in same skillet over medium-high heat. Add chicken; cook 5 minutes per side or until browned. Place chicken in **CROCK-POT®** slow cooker.

3. Pour broth into skillet. Cook and stir over medium-high heat, scraping up any browned bits from bottom of skillet. Pour broth mixture into **CROCK-POT®** slow cooker. Add tomatoes, raisins, curry powder, salt, paprika and black pepper. Cover; cook on **LOW 3 hours.** Serve chicken and sauce over rice. Garnish with parsley.

makes 4 servings

Stuffed Chicken Breasts

6 boneless, skinless chicken breasts

8 ounces feta cheese, crumbled

3 cups chopped fresh spinach leaves

⅓ cup oil-packed sun-dried tomatoes, drained and chopped

1 teaspoon minced lemon peel

1 teaspoon dried basil, oregano or mint

½ teaspoon garlic powder

Black pepper

1 can (about 14 ounces) diced tomatoes

½ cup oil-cured olives*

Hot cooked polenta

*If using pitted olives, add to slow cooker in final hour of cooking.

1. Place chicken breast between 2 pieces of plastic wrap. Using tenderizer mallet or back of skillet, pound breast until about ¼ inch thick. Repeat with remaining chicken.

2. Combine feta, spinach, sun-dried tomatoes, lemon peel, basil, garlic powder and pepper in medium bowl.

3. Lay pounded chicken, smooth side down, on work surface. Place about 2 tablespoons feta mixture on wide end of breast. Roll up tightly. Repeat with remaining chicken.

4. Place rolled chicken, seam side down, in **CROCK-POT**® slow cooker. Top with diced tomatoes and olives. Cover; cook on **LOW 5½ to 6 hours** or on **HIGH 4 hours.** Serve over polenta.

makes 6 servings

Chinese Cashew Chicken

1 can (16 ounces) bean sprouts, drained

2 cups sliced cooked chicken

1 can (10¾ ounces) condensed cream of mushroom soup, undiluted

1 cup sliced celery

½ cup chopped green onions

1 can (4 ounces) sliced mushrooms, drained

3 tablespoons butter

1 tablespoon soy sauce

1 cup whole cashews

Hot cooked rice

1. Combine bean sprouts, chicken, soup, celery, green onions, mushrooms, butter and soy sauce in **CROCK-POT®** slow cooker; mix well. Cover; cook on **LOW 4 to 6 hours** or on **HIGH 2 to 3 hours.**

2. Stir in cashews just before serving. Serve over rice.

makes 4 servings

Tip: For easier preparation, cut up the ingredients for this **CROCK-POT®** slow cooker recipe the night before. Wrap the chicken and vegetables separately, and store in the refrigerator. Do not place the stoneware in the refrigerator.

Nice 'n' Easy Italian Chicken

4 boneless, skinless chicken breasts (about 1 pound)
8 ounces mushrooms, sliced
1 medium green bell pepper, chopped
1 medium zucchini, diced
1 medium onion, chopped
1 jar (26 ounces) pasta sauce
   Hot cooked linguini or spaghetti

Combine all ingredients except linguini in **CROCK-POT®** slow cooker. Cover; cook on **LOW 6 to 8 hours** or until chicken is tender. Serve over linguini.

makes 4 servings

Continental Chicken

1 package (2¼-ounces) dried beef, cut into pieces
4 boneless, skinless chicken breasts (about 1-pound)
4 slices bacon
1 can (10¾-ounces) condensed cream of mushroom soup, undiluted
¼ cup all-purpose flour
¼ cup sour cream
   Hot cooked noodles

1. Coat **CROCK-POT®** slow cooker with nonstick cooking spray. Place dried beef in bottom. Wrap each chicken breast with one bacon slice. Place wrapped chicken on top of dried beef.

2. Combine soup and flour in medium bowl until smooth. Pour over chicken. Cover; cook on **LOW 7 to 8 hours** or on **HIGH 3 to 4 hours.**

3. Place sour cream in small bowl; stir in a few tablespoons of cooking liquid from **CROCK-POT®** slow cooker. Stir sour cream mixture into remaining cooking liquid. Cover; cook on **LOW 5 minutes** or until heated through. Serve chicken and sauce over noodles.

makes 4 servings